Taking My Letters Back

New and Selected Poems

DERMOT BOLGER

New Island Books
Dublin

TAKING MY LETTERS BACK
First published 1998 by
New Island Books
2 Brookside
Dundrum Road
Dublin 14
Ireland

British Library Cataloguing in Publication Data
A catalogue record for this book is available from the British Library

ISBN 1 874597 98 7

Grant-aided by the
Arts Council

New Island Books receives financial assistance from The Arts
Council (An Chomhairle Ealaíon), Ireland.

Cover design: Slick Fish Design, Dublin
Cover photograph: Steve Pyke
Typesetting: New Island Books
Printed in Ireland by Colour Books Ltd.

Contents

Acknowledgments are made to the editors of the following where certain of these poems appeared: *Soho Square* (Bloomsbury, London & Faber, USA), *The Forward Book of Poetry, 1995*, *The Crab Orchard Review* (Southern Illinois University at Carbondale), *The Cimarron Review* (University of Oklahoma), *New Orleans Review* (Loyola, New Orleans University), *The Literary Review* (Fairleigh Dickinson University, New Jersey), *The New Poetry* (Bloodaxe), *Thumbscrew* (Oxford), *Favourite Poems of Ireland* (Mercier Press), *At the Year's Turning* (Dedalus Press), *The Younger Irish Poets* (Blackstaff), *My Generation* (Lilliput Press), *Rochefort, Veus d'aealleups* (France), *Irish Poetry Now* (Wolfhound), *Irish Love Poems* (O'Brien Press), *InCognito*, RTÉ, The BBC, Oxford University Press (Canada) and *The Irish Times*.

A special thanks to Aengus Fanning, editor of *The Sunday Independent*, Dublin, where over two dozen of these poems appeared, and to Willie Kealy and Campbell Spray for their care and attention.

'The Lament for Arthur Cleary' – which takes its starting point from '*Caoineadh Airt Uí Laoghaire*', the lament for her husband by Eibhlín Dubh Ní Chonaill – was first published by Mr Ciaran Carty in the *Sunday Tribune* and later published in *Internal Exiles*. It was later rewritten as a play of the same title by the author, who is grateful to the judges of the Samuel Beckett Award, The Stewart Parker BBC Prize and the Edinburgh Fringe First Awards, which the play received.

The collection *Internal Exiles* was published by The Dolmen Press. *Leinster Street Ghosts, No Waiting America, Finglas Lilies* and *The Habit of Flesh* were published by Raven Arts Press.

for Sheila Fitzgerald,
Colm Hewitt
and
Anthony Cronin;
first readers,
with thanks.

I: Brevities: New Poems (1994-98)

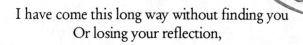

Prayer

I have come this long way without finding you
      Or losing your reflection,

And tried a dozen obsessions without cleansing
      Your taste from my tongue.

Oldest friend and adversary, fugitive brother,
      We recognise each other

In carriages of express trains which pass:
      Your hands beat on the glass.

1997

Wherever You Woke

There only ever was one street,
    One back garden, one bedroom:
Wherever you woke you woke beneath

    The ceiling where you were born,
For the briefest unconscious second
    An eyelid's flutter from home.

1994

Lines for an Unknown Uncle

(i.m. Francis Bolger, died 3rd June, 1928)

No son or granddaughter to remember:
    No trace of your seventeen years left,
Except in the mind of a younger brother

    Sent out onto the street to wait,
While you screamed in the height of fever
    For someone to finish you with an axe.

1998

Release

It is time to exhume, mark mourning's demise:
  To gather as survivors, remove the lid

And discover, teeming between skull and rib,
  Redeeming shoals of rainbow butterflies.

1994

14

II

from
The Habit of Flesh
1980

Having Never Run Away

I

Having never run away from home,
I could only imagine the pain
    Of hiding under some hedgerow,
Beneath one streetlamp down a lane,
    Using my school bag as a pillow
While my comics smudged in the rain.

    My mother would be waiting
For a squad car to ferry me back
    To the bustling police station
Where she would cradle my head,
    Our quarrel resolved as I returned
To the drowsy cocoon of my bed.

II

Now I walk home
From some hazy party,
The streets freeze,
Leaves blow past me.

The house is empty.
I search for a light switch
And realise that home
Has run away from me.

1977

The Lady in the Fields

(or *Sending My Letters*)

(For S.F.)

I

The first night in your caravan I screamed
   And woke in unaccustomed dark,
Listening to sounds across the fields
   Of wind and cattle and a dog's bark.

Your breakfast table grew cluttered
   As books and memories laid siege
To the food we forgot to eat,
   Rocking in the tides of the breeze.

We startled foxes in your forest sanctuary
   Where hard-drinking in-laws had ruled
From a Big House now tangled in creepers
   That curtain green-lit crumbling rooms.

Later we climbed the Mayo hills
   To an old man with hordes of cats
Who conjured spirits in his smoky cabin,
   Beneath dripping, moss-stained thatch.

That night we talked by candlelight,
   Sipping foreign scented teas,
Till dawn broke the hymen of night
   And tongues spoke effortlessly.

At half-six we woke in rain
   To the cries of a stray cat,
Instinctively crawling to your door
   After a car crushed his back.

You gathered him up in your arms,
  Fingering his broken bones,
Then guided him towards death,
  Peacefully breathing in chloroform.

While I dug a grave in the field
  You laid him in an old blanket
And said you would stop having pets,
  There was too much suffering in it.

II

  Thank you for your letter.
You say the snow has finally gone,
  The moon is orange and full,
Transfixing your field into an Eden.

  Four cats live in a basket
And respect the birds who come,
  And live with sheep who rub
Winter coats against your door.

 In the frozen dawn food appears
For all your sheltering friends,
  Who return to you with wounds
That your trust slowly mends.

  Old woman, kindling my mind:
You live out what others write,
  A solitary lamp in dark fields,
An Ark sailing through the night.

Mayo/Dublin, 1977

III

Four lives from
Finglas Lilies
1981

Finglas Lilies

(Frankie's story)

I: The party, June 1977

A girl lies on the grass,
Beyond the lights of houses,
    With dew soaking her back.

Flocks of leaves swarm
Above her like water lilies
    Over a sunken garden.

Dawn forms like stubble:
An unshaven morning surfaces,
    Jaded and looking for trouble.

Her hair is tangled as seaweed,
Salty and drenched to touch.
    Like the song of clubbed seals,

Her scared cry pushes them apart,
As he withdraws too late inside her
    And dreams seep into the grass.

II: London, Autumn 1977

A tiny flat in North London,
    They live on frozen food,
Make friends across the landing.

At night she often cries.
   They make love softly
For fear of harming the child

Developing like a negative
   In the pit of her stomach.
They finally call her relatives.

On the night crossing Dublin rose
   Like a curtain over a window
Riddled with bullet holes.

III: Finglas, 1979

Steel winds at dawn sting like a wasp,
   In this factory where men curse
And rust grows like hair on a corpse.

She's off to work as he finishes night shift.
   Today is their child's first birthday,
They'll put his name on the housing list.

Taking a chair he sits in the garden,
   Smoking Moroccan dope and tripping,
The housing estate keeps disappearing.

He feels himself at the bottom of a pond,
   Floating below rows of water lilies
With new names like Finglas and Ballymun.

1980

Captain of a Space Ship

(Tom Casey, poet of Ballymun's tower blocks)

"I pace upon the battlements and stare." W.B. Yeats

I: *Morning*

Below concrete clouds,
On a level with my eyes,
   The seagulls cry
With white electric noise.

   I watch from the balcony
Of this high-rise tower block
   Roads quiet as veins
When blood has stopped.

It's freezing at this hour
   As I huddle in my coat,
Captain of a space ship
   Which never got afloat.

When the first bus moves
   From its terminus,
Sweet God of Morning
   Look down on us

Who watch from balconies
   The cars, lane by lane,
Flashing past at speed
   Through this fertility farm,

Or lovers skipping school,
    Flitting into back fields
Beyond Corporation estates
    For a smoke and a tease.

I sent them the love
    Of my seventy years,
But it's my experience
    That I need to share.

At this table all night
    I tried to find words
For the wounds of Liverpool
    To somehow be cured,

Or doss houses in Scotland,
    Or drying out in The Smoke.
I fed them my life-story,
    But the words never spoke.

II: *Evening*

At half-five this evening
    A child climbed on a ledge,
Her face like a slapped arse,
    Red with cold as she fell.

A space capsule trailing
    A parachute of skirt,
Exploded as it re-entered
    The tarmacadamed earth.

The knot of rush-hour traffic,
    Collared on the roundabout
Like a cobra eating itself,
    Seemed untouched by the fallout.

Her mother, late from work,
    Was climbing the beanstalk
To their tenth-storey flat,
    Because the lifts were broke.

I watch from this balcony,
    My throat and palms are dry,
But my eyes are bloodshot
    And gaze towards the sky.

III: *Night*

Later, alone in my bedroom,
    When I turned out the light,
Ribs of coathangers shivered
    Like teeth in the night.

Noise from the flats downstairs
    Drifted around me as I lay,
Like a plug that had fused,
    Like the word becoming clay.

At such times I must imagine
    How it will be when it comes,
Like rain's tapping to the deaf
    Or sudden language to the dumb,

Or blind eyes glimpsing
    The thousand shades of morning
Watching from my crow's nest
    For the land that keeps calling

Through a gap in the shutters
    I see my space ship dock,
In clusters of green lights
    It hovers by the tower block.

Every night from this table
    I climb on board verse-craft;
Crystal phrases ignite my mind
    And steer me through the dark.

1980/81

Skinhead Song

Brute force and ignorance
   On streets at closing time,
Violence throbs like a drill
   Splintering apart my spine.

A thin contour is carved
   Across a bouncer's face,
A map of hatred comes alive
   As blood bubbles to escape.

The world sparkles like cider:
   Through the streets I float,
All night this city sleeps
   In terror of bovver boots.

Until dawn takes on the shade
   Of filthy chip-shop grease
Stiffening so fast around me
   That I scream for release.

'Brute Force & Ignorance'
   Plays on inside my mind
Like a needle on scratched vinyl,
   While I get left behind

By crowds walking to work,
   Through another bus strike,
Leaving me on this estate
   Of hatchet-faced housewives.

1981

'Brute Force & Ignorance' is a song by Rory Gallagher

Aisling Fionn Ghlas

(Allison's story)

One morning with sunlight
 You burst upon my life,
In your brother's house
 Locked out for the night.

His door creaking open,
 Hands searching for gloves,
The snap-shock of waking,
 To behold you, my love.

From his window I watched
 You move, so compact,
Your slender body tightened
 Up by the act

Of bending down to tie
 A small dog's rein,
At fifteen, in taut jeans,
 In a Finglas lane.

In a factory in England
 On night-shift, looking back,
I'd see your body emerging
 From that cul-de-sac

Reflected by the steel moon
 In a guttered pool of rain,
Your smile over my machine
 Marked morning again.

Gentle as a Japanese lady,
    With slow dignity,
Pregnant for the third time,
    Two years married:

I called your name by the shops
    The day I came home,
Your smile when you turned
    Was swathed in Valium.

1980

IV

from
No Waiting America
1982

Stardust Sequence

(i.m. those young people killed by fire after emergency exits were chained in the Stardust Night Club, a converted jam factory, Artane, North Dublin, 1982)

I

Shadows whisper a new language of possibilities
From hidden couples reminding us we are not alone
In searching for romance and the kinship encountered
While dancing to the secret tongues of our peers.
Through steel shutters clamped across windows
Rock music invents a vocabulary that unites us.

Strobelights on the ceiling break up the air until
The brain keeps pace with the body's theatricality
In this slow, fragmented black-and-white movie.
Every Friday you would dance away the hours
In gathering tempo until the harsh glare of bulbs
Evicted you from a space that was briefly yours.

Thrust out into the night you'd doss or go home
Among couples & groups of girls singing of love.
But tomorrow you will wander incubator estates
And stare disbelieving, in the brutality of dawn,
At silent families maintaining vigils in doorways
With only numb anger left burning inside them.

II

Last night in swirling colour we danced again,
And, as Strobelights stunned in black & white,
I reached in this agony of slow motion for you.
But you danced on as if cold light still shone,
Merging into the crowd as my path was blocked
By snarling bouncers & dead-eyed club owners.

When I screamed across the music nobody heard,
I flailed under spotlights like a disco dancer
And people formed a circle clapping to the beat
As I shuddered round the club in a violent fit.
Hurtling through a dream without trembling awake,
I revolved through space until I hit the ground.

Lying among their feet tramping out the tunes,
I grasped you inside my mind for this moment,
Your white dress bobbing in a cool candle- flame,
Illuminating the darkness spinning towards me:
A teenage dancing queen, proud of her footwork,
Sparks rising like stardust all over the floor.

III

We are here along the edge of people's memories,
A reference point in the calendar of their lives.
Our absence linked with acceptances or refusals
On summer evenings when love seemed attainable
And moist lips opened after dances in the parks.
We are the unavoidable stillbirth of your past.

That golden girl you loved, pregnant at seventeen;
Young friends growing sour, paralysed by the dole;
Your senile boss, already rotting inside his skin,
Returns the look of hatred that's burning you up,
Drawing new breath from every young life wrecked.
All those smooth men who would quietly forget us,

Who turn you on a spit over cold flames of dissent,
Are guilty of murder as if they chained the exits
When we stampeded through their illusion of order.
We have buried in your skull these ashes of doubt
And you believe nothing but one slow fuse of anger
Since the night your thin candle of youth ran out.

IV: Survivors

(Lines written on the discovery of a child's incorrupt
corpse, long buried in a Irish graveyard)

child saint coffined in her vacuum of earth   mercuried
blood clogging dried veins   a single eye stupidly open
stagnant skin incorrupt   inhuman

these wasted years while a century unfolded here nothing
happened   now let earth creak through   trickle of
clay   blind inquisitiveness of worms

until in this wooden box
under a crust of earth   her skin bubbles
in slow motion into blisters of decay

let rib and skull emerge like this sleeping girl's flesh
gleaming through dark into dawn   as I learn to
touch the scars that surgery left
the seam of stitches she tried to hide:

do not shiver as if my fingers were ice   open your
eyes loosely into the risks of day   without mourning
your miracle of survival

pity those souls crippled
through fear of the knife's continuing life   the uncom-
promising worms' teeth promising eternity

1982

My Head Buried . . .

My head buried in the sanctuary of your hair,
I see you pass beneath trees on a blonde morning
To enter the gates of the Hospice for the Dying.

Behind screens your patient has fretted since dawn,
Sensing her pulse fade along the blue flex of veins
Criss-crossing her frayed wrists that beat for attention.

She stares at the sunlight like an apparition,
With naked feet chafing against the bedstead,
Dying in the terrible shadow of God's promise.

You do not shirk from arms drawing you down
To the withered lips of her child-like frame,
Your kiss rinsed away her vigil of loneliness.

I raise my head till your black hair rustles back.
Shaking, I hold you and your lips part under mine:
Your pupils still reflect that woman's final breath

As she saw life in them dissolve into blind trust:
Its seed carried from her in a sepal of spittle
That blossoms when our tongues slowly touch.

1982

V

from
Internal Exiles
1986

Two Labouring Men

I: Matt Talbot, 1856-1925

I need to rinse out the rancid can you drank from
In a ramshackled shed beside the timber yard gates,

To place a mattress over the plank you slept on
And release rusted dog chains from your waist.

We have each sobered awake in the abyss of dawn,
Longing for a revelation to overwhelm our futility,

But you substituted torture with an addict's fixation
That ensnared us in the servitude of poverty.

Lift your head, Matt, and read on the newsboys' placards
How Dublin burns as you trudge each evening from work

To shuffle to your meal on bare knees across floorboards,
With blunt labourer's eyes out-staring those who mock,

Until you fall in Gramby Lane, missing your final Mass,
Like you carried the whole city's pain upon your back.

1986

II: Robert Tressell, 1870–1911

Always they were conquistadors with blood-axes glinting,
Or dour agents storing grain in the ravages of famine,
Until you revealed a second wretched English nation
Concealed behind Grand Parade in the slums of Hastings,
By masters who were no more their countrymen than mine.

Terrified you might remove their children's right to serve
And queue in ragged trousers to undersell their labour,
Puffed by Sunday School, stale bread and lies of grandeur,
They mocked your notion that they could shape the future
As they idled in the cancer of one more starving winter.

Robert Tressell, tonight I see a cart being pushed by men
Up a steep hill, loaded with ladders and paint cans,
And you, tubercular, in broken boots, coughing up blood
As you shoved your way homeward to shape the novel
You would never live to see pound out in letterpress.

The red sun you walk towards has not been extinguished.
Beyond the trials and gulags of this shattered century
Its spell glows as strong as when you wrote till dawn,
A dying man in penury, warmed only by your vision
Of future children growing in your "*risen sun of socialism*".

1986

The Watcher's Agony

I: Ghosts in the Ark

Just before we slept your tongue crept into my mouth,
I dreamt inside its aftertaste of a tide sifting out.
When I woke I was terrified you were taken from me,
I pressed against your body, waking you in my urgency.

The room overhead seemed filled by the arms of men
From a foreign city in your dream, holding you down again.
Your body shuddered feeling mine, lost between worlds,
And you gazed at me, fearfully, not knowing who I was.

In your eyes I could feel myself, exhausted and anxious,
But occluded from the memories that set your brain adrift.
The future balanced as I tried to still your restlessness,

And, in my failure, the past crashed against our tiny ark.
Now, whenever you open yourself to me, old pain rushes in,
And ghosts hover like vultures, waiting to claim you back.

February, 1983

II: The Watcher's Agony

The devil is in this room tonight. He wants us.
Cups rattle in your mind and the table levitates.

I hold onto your body as if trying to protect you,
But the terror trapped in your imagination escapes.

Can you hear a word I say or even feel my presence?
I cannot grasp what is disintegrating under my arms

Where you shudder, wedging yourself into my shoulder,
Then speak in a voice estranged from your own.

The devil is in this room tonight. Inside both of us:
Everything we ever suppressed attacks the furniture.

When I black out into sleep I dream I am still awake
And you lean above me, choking on words I cannot hear.

This flat has broken loose from the moorings of reality,
It pitches and rolls through the tempest in your mind.

The devil you see, frantically tugging the smashed helm,
As he turns, wild-eyed in the spray, is his face mine?

March, 1983

Pearse Triptych

I: Renunciation: P.H. Pearse

(After P.H. Pearse's poem, 'Renunciation')

Naked I saw thee, sweet beauty beyond beauty,
 But I blinded my eyes for fear I would fail.
My palms were dry and my racked body shivering,
 When I screamed awake from her teasing laughter.

> *no longer can I feel my face under this second skin:*
> *they have fused together under rain and baked in*
>   *the heat*
> *of platforms where my voice invented a nation to live in,*
> *among haunted eyes staring from the faces of defeat.*

Christ, I see Thee in Thy rituals and certainty,
 Shield me in the confines of Your lonely march;
My mind knows the fever of a barefoot boy's kiss,
 Let the wafer of Your loins slacken my thirst.

> *armed men believe I command them, but they lead me*
> *out of myself, into this role where I may express,*
> *by a million doves of flame released over the town,*
> *how, when the heart cannot open, it must burn down.*

1983

II: The Five Re-Tellings Of Iosagan

(*After P.H. Pearse's story, 'Iosagan'*)

V

There's the spot where Matthew saw The Stranger appear,
Playing among other children with a halo of sun in His hair,
And here's the priest's door where one night The Boy came
And led him to hear Matthew's first confession in thirty
    years,
Before the old man died, calling in wonder Iosagan's name.

VI

Some say a Boy appeared to him while the village was at
    Mass
And, though the old man tried to tell them, nobody would
    believe.
That night Matthew ran from the woods, crying Our Lord's
    name
My grandfather said you could hear music like angels in the
    breeze.

III

Some boy did vanish from the Galway workhouse that
    summer,
But I remember Matthew as a harmless gobshite simpleton.
Whenever I'd sit on his knee he'd gibber about angels
    appearing.

II

Trees reeling in terror and his heart seizing up as he falls,
Clutching the priest's skirt, screaming "*It was The Lamb of God*".

I

A shrivelled foreskin smeared with blood, semen and shit.

1984

III: Lullaby of a Woman of the Flats

(after P.H. Pearse's 'Lullaby of a Woman of the Mountains')

Small fragile head, my life's precious candle,
I will guard your sleep before longings claim you.

Smeared hungry mouth that my breast has known,
You will taste the white milk of heroin and flour.

Flushed crimson cheeks, before stubble can harden,
Apostles of violence will brand their caste onto you.

Powdered milk of death besieging my baby's mouth,
This city's ashen hands anointing his cheeks!

Flats, be still, and insatiable hungers that gnaw
Stay banished inside your lair of television tubes.

Cars, below the balconies, deaden your engines,
Flashed blades of speed, silence your beckoning.

Siren and gun-shot, do not echo through my home,
Chords of wanderlust do not taunt him to come.

Phantoms of our age that call in the night-time,
Do not stir tonight till cursed streets whiten.

1984

1966

"*The bells of the midday Angelus, ringing over Dublin this Easter Sunday, will carry, as well as a call to prayer, a special note of triumph and joy benefiting the occasion of the Golden Jubilee of the Rising of 1916, that is being marked with pageantry and spectacle.*"

Irish Press, 10th April 1966.

An ordered ocean of flags swaying at dawn,
We shall march forth to meet with destiny.

Gold banners between houses in every town,
We shall march forth to meet with destiny.

Their medals glinting in the ageing ranks,
The survivors marched past the monuments,
Faces proud and stiff in each camera lens:
We shall march forth to meet with destiny.

An ordered sea of feet among littered bread,
We shall march forth to meet with destiny.

Gulls shriek as teachers drill us into step,
We shall march forth to meet with destiny.

We paraded in line towards the wooden desks,
Past a framed proclamation and a crucifix,
And begged God that our turn would be next:
We shall march forth to meet with destiny.

A tide of rhetoric flooding the platforms,
We shall march forth to meet with destiny.

Engraining a call to duty into our bones,
We shall march forth to meet with destiny.

Images of trapped men racing through flame
Left the incomplete ache of a phantom pain,
But through our blood they would be freed
When we marched forth to meet with destiny.

We would march forth to meet with destiny.

1986

Dublin Girl, Mountjoy Jail, 1984

I dreamt it all, from end to end, the carriageway,
The rivulet behind the dairy streaked with crystal,
A steel moon glinting in a guttered stream of rain,
And the steep hill that I would crest to find her,
My child asleep in my old bedroom beside my sister.

I dreamt it all, and when I woke, furtive girls
Were clambering onto the bars of the windows,
White shapes waving against the dark skyline,
Praying for hands to reply from the men's cells
Before screws broke up the vigil of handkerchiefs.

I dreamt it all, the times I swore never again
To walk that carriageway, a rivulet of heroin glowing
In my veins until I shivered in its aftertaste,
And hid with my child in the closed-down factory
Where my brain snapped like a brittle fingernail.

I dreamt it all, the longing to touch her, the seance
In the cell when we screamed at the picture falling,
The warmth of circled hands after the frozen glass
Between my child and me, a warder following her words
To be rationed out and lived off for days afterwards.

I dreamt of you, who means all to me, my daughter,
How we might run to that carriageway by the rivulet,
And, when I woke, a blue pupil was patrolling my sleep,
Jailing my dreams in the vacant orbit of its world,
Narrowed down to a spyhole, a globed eyelid closing.

1984

The Futures Market

Wind rattles the window frames and the floorboards rot.
It's been eight days since I stepped beyond this filthy flat
Where I sit watching and four times my vigil has been
   rewarded.

Four times I've hung within the limbo of static on the
   screen,
Longing for release, yet not daring to believe it could
   happen,
And four times the picture hasn't jerked back to
   advertisements:

My throat has turned dry and my hands trembled as I
   watched
The figure thrown naked into the room and the beating
   begin.
Whole days wither in this flat when nothing
   happens,

Days when I'm stuck like an insect on fly paper unable to
   move,
Trapped within cyberspace in a meteorite shower of static
Where I wait and pray the advertisements will not continue

As over and over they repeat without commentary or
   pity,
Hammering out slogans at those remaining sealed in our
   rooms.
Once we walked down streets and worked in throbbing
   factories,

I remember oil on my overalls and the smell of sweat
  without fear,
But then governments collapsed and reformed and were
  submerged
By corporations who had learnt how to function without us.

Just four times the knife has flashed like a matador's
And youngsters raised their heads, though blinded by the
  hood.
There's no way of knowing how many of my workmates are
  left,

Caged before crackling screens, terrified to miss each
  murder.
Yesterday I saw a man with a plastic bag run through the
  litter,
Apart from him all streets were deserted to the superstore.

I breathe safely – I'm too old for anybody's attention,
They will never come to shove me hooded into a studio,
I won't strain my head forward in expectation of the blow.

From my final refuge I can spy on their agony;
The flesh wincing and their final anonymous pain.
Afterwards I breathe again in my renewed triumph of
  surviving.

Nobody knows any longer when the curfew begins or ends
But one evening I heard them come for someone on this
  street.
I never knew which hooded neighbour I had once passed

Kept all of us contained for a day with his death.
They are killing me too in this war of nerves,
It's been years since I've not slept upright in a chair,

Dreaming of blood and waking fretfully to advertisements.
Yet still I cling on, speaking to nobody in the superstore,
Running home frantic I will miss a final glimpse of life.

Long ago I believed in God – now I believe what I am told:
There is no heaven except the instant when the set comes
    alive,

No purgatory except infinite static bombarding the screen,
Hell could only be if they came for the television or for me.

1983

Amsterdam

He woke up at once and there was nothing he could feel,
He switched on the light to make sure the girl had gone,
The night air was humming like a shot had just torn it,
He washed in ice-cold water and put his business suit on.

The cocaine was strapped in bandages across his ribcage,
The briefcase's false handle opened just to his touch,
He took a taxi from the hotel and the driver was singing,
Airport officials nodded as he strode through the crush.

If he could feel anything he would remember dreaming
Of that taxi ride which seemed about to bring him home,
But always turned instead down a narrow walled road
To stop amid ranks of tombstones in a lifting grey dawn.

'This is as far as you take me. This is it,' he spoke finally.
'You catch on faster than most,' the waiting driver replied.
But already he has forgotten as his plane glides through
    clouds,
He stares through Ray-bans at the earth rolling to one side.

1984

'Bob Marley Lives'

The wall by the fire station bears your legend
    In scrawled metallic red lettering,

And young girls gathered in the park at dusk
    Listen to your Jamaican voice singing.

I cross the arched skeleton of a pedestrian bridge
    Where boys with guitar cases wait,

And under glistening dreadlocks of a burst main
    Weekend hordes of children celebrate.

Water lashes out like an overwhelmed teacher
    As they dodge his dissolving thongs,

And the pulse of your music threads every vein
    Of a new nation awkwardly being born,

As you help us still to sing new songs of freedom,
    Over Dublin streets, redemption songs.

1985

White Shirts in Childhood

White shirts in the wardrobe were hovering souls
Who fluttered in the darkness at my shoulder
And in dreams a woman descended the stairs,
To where I cowered by the locked front door.
Worms slithered beneath her feet on each step,
As I woke, convinced they littered the mattress,
And ran to the tortured eyes of the Scared Heart
To pray with my cheek against the cold glass.

Tonight, when I dreamt death was imminent,
I stood defiant at that door, gazing up the stairs,
Challenging an unknown woman to finally appear:
But only a haunted silence tapped out: *You are alone.*
I awoke without the prospect of ghosts in the dark
And pressed my cheek helplessly to your photograph.

1985

Bluebells for Grainne

Through the shuttered light of the blinking trees we race,
Then the van rounds the corner into a sleeping hamlet
Where we climb down, light-headed from late night drinking,
For a final stop before our work together is finished.

The old driver arranges flowers in the folds of your dress
As we laze against a sunlit wall, indulgent in this day
That glides like a kite we finger lightly to keep afloat,
Trailing shimmering tails of all our future hopes.

Often our brains baked beneath a crust of officialdom,
Yet we kept each other sane by learning how to hum
Subversive songs of friendship that flowered underneath
Schedules commanding us to vanish in a swirl of dust.

When it settles, remember me, grinning idiotically up at you
In a spring dress, with bluebells spilling from your breast.

The mobile library, St. Margaret's Village, 1984

VI

The Lament for Arthur Cleary
1985

The Lament for Arthur Cleary

My lament for you, Arthur Cleary,
  As you lay down that crooked back lane,
Under the stern wall of a factory
  Where moss and crippled flowers cling

To stone crested by glass and wire,
  With a runlet of blood down your chest
When I raced screaming towards you,
  Hearing their cluster of boots retreat.

I cupped your face in my palms
  To taste life draining from your lips
And you died attempting to smile
  As defiant and proud as you had lived.

Behind me I could hear the cry
  Of an engine kick-starting to life
And vanishing through laneways
  Where we had rode on autumn nights.

May it have led them mesmerised
  Beneath railway bridges to the river
And skidded over oily cobbles
  To drown those who killed its master.

You were the only man I knew,
  The rest were all dancing clones,
Lions swaggering in packs,
  Kittens petrified on their own,

Unable to glance at a girl
  Unless cocky with drink or stoned.

But you stared into my face,
　　Caught in the strobe lights alone,

Not leering or smart-arsed,
　　Nor mumbling like a blushing bride,
Leading me to the dance floor
　　Where firm hands brushed my thighs.

Confettied light combed our faces
　　From spinning globes of speckled mirrors
When we walked towards the exit
　　Through those swirling ranks of dancers,

Beyond the cajoling disc jockey
　　And nervous girls trying to look bored,
Away from the slow crucifixions
　　I'd witnessed stranded on that floor.

Our ears still humming with static
　　We moved out into the tense nightscape,
Past the crumpled stalks of drunks
　　Falling between the dispersed sheaves

Of crowds swept from discotheques,
　　The glazed lovers with no place to stay
Queuing under the gaze of bouncers
　　In O'Connell Street's honky-tonk cafés.

Sombre patriots and liberators
　　Stood paralysed in bird-stained bronze
While you unchained your motor-bike
　　And gave me your helmet to put on.

I accepted it like a pledge
　　And my arms circled your leather jacket,

Your hair blown into my face,
   We raced up the quays towards my estate.

Down a lane choked with scrap,
   Hidden by rust-eaten ghosts of lorries,
Within sight of my father's house,
   Is where I first loved Arthur Cleary.

With gems of shattered glass
   Sparkling in light from gypsy caravans,
I unpeeled my black sweater
   And felt a nipple harden on his tongue.

Deserted streets had lightened
   Before I undressed in exhilaration,
And lay jaded beside my window
   To catch the first blue notes of dawn,

That blurred into whiteness
   Where he lay curled against my back,
His limbs clambering onto me
   Until I woke by myself sopping wet.

                    *

My lament for Arthur Cleary
   And the life he tried to lead,
Taking what jobs suited him,
   Contemptuous of all permanency.

From the final generation
   To have always known a start
In factory or timber yard,
   Who moved as work grew slack.

Those born in our new winter
    Are taught terror from birth
And moulded like plasticine
    Into the first ensnaring niche,

Or are defeated early on
    By the propaganda of despair,
And chalk days off in blood
    On the city's eternal corners.

They'd run to the flats
    With plunder in their arms
From derelict car parks,
    Pursued by whirling sirens.

We ignored questioning
    And watched from your bike
The squad cars retreat
    And shaven heads strut out,

Tempted by a fraction
    Of the value from a fence,
Black-booted tribesmen
    Shivering for their fix,

Their youth suffocated
    In the famine of poppies
Spreading in the dust
    Blown down concrete steps,

With geriatric faces
    Screwed up in bright light,
Watching for the car
    To slow at the entrance

And the hand to appear
   Dispensing white packages
From a darkened window
   Before the driver accelerates.

I had a room with fresh linen
   And parents to watch over me,
A brown dog slept at my feet,
   I left them for Arthur Cleary,

To climb that steep aisle
   Scrawled with lover's graffiti,
Where only genuflecting gulls
   Swooped to witness our ceremony.

Flocks of children swarmed
   Along the cliffedge of doorways,
Women called to each other
   From tiers of laundered balconies,

Through the blare of radios,
   Noise of soccer and girls jeering
From those honeycombed steps,
   Till dusk announced Friday evening

And furtive parents withdrew
   To sit in unlit rooms with children,
Who waited, terrified to move,
   For the arrogant hammering to begin.

Behind walls we sensed them
   Like Jews hidden in compartments,
Hearing a money-lender's knuckles
   Scrape at their taut nerve ends.

*

Languid in its afterglow,
    We lay in positions love left us,
Watching a pane of light
    Slide over the moonlit furniture,

And then you would whisper
    All those place names of Europe,
Like a litany of ex-lovers
    Whom distance had made mythical.

I'd see dawn over Holland
    Where you laboured in a factory
And watched whitening skylights
    Mark another shift's completion.

Or long rows of branches
    Stretching down Danish orchards,
And three ribs cracked
    In a strike of foreign pickers.

Sunday mornings in Hamburg,
    Down the steps at Jungfernstieg,
Feeding bread from a booth
    To swans splashing on the river,

Or homesick that afternoon,
    Wandering through the Reeperbahn
Past neon striptease signs
    Where girls hustle in spitting rain.

Often I lose sight of you,
    Boarding a U-Bahn at Hauptbahnhof,
Shunted in a swaying tube
    To a dour migrant workers' hostel,

And mounting the third bunk
  In the stink of Turkish cigarettes
To stare at Dublin's streets
  Tattooed along veins on your wrist.

Or halted at a border post,
  Pulling a compartment window down
To watch the guard's light
  Flicker on the wheels of the train.

Clutching your green passport
  In a limbo between foreign states,
Consumed with nostalgia
  For an identity irretrievably lost,

Which you tried to reclaim,
  Like the heir returned to an estate
Of hulks of gutted streets
  Being demolished for parking space,

Where bulldozers advanced,
  Flanked by a flotilla of children,
Scutting onto the safety frames
  In a grim carnival of destruction.

On your new motorbike   ·
  In the April days after we met,
I would slip my hands
  Into the warmth of your jacket

And watch blurred tar
  Spin backwards beneath us,
As we rode past Ballymun
  Through a green maze of tunnels

Crazily paved with light,
   Shaken from overlapping branches,
Bordering the twisting roads
   That swept downwards to Skerries.

If I ignored the dichotomy
   Between your words and what I saw,
It was because my pulse thrilled
   In the slipstream of your world.

But that world had died,
   Though you could not realise it,
A grey smudge of estates
   Charted the encroaching horizon

Whose listless children,
   Staring you down when we passed,
Were the future forming
   Behind windscreens of stolen cars.

Gone were the fistfights
   And the flash of steel combs,
The bolted flats sweated
   Under the reign of shotguns,

As you drew your legacy
   In a Victorian labour exchange
And saw every old friend
   Succumb to emigration or jail.

*

Grief is a knot
   That is choking my throat,

Rage is a whirlwind
   Imploding through my skull.

If only I had known
   Your life to be in danger
I would have clawed
   My way between you and them.

I would have bitten
   Into their skin with my teeth,
I would have stubbed
   Out their eyes with my nails.

If only I had shouted
   When you walked from the flat,
Or ran to the balcony,
   Still naked, to call you back.

You went down steps
   Because the lift was broken,
You paused outside
   And strolled out of my life,

Across a courtyard
   Where housewives were talking,
Lying between sheets
   I could hear the engine start.

I drifted into sleep
   To see a horse come riderless
Over fields trailing
   A bridle smeared with blood,

Towards a white house
   Where a woman stood screaming,

As I shuddered awake
   I realised her voice was mine.

I ran into the street
   Where small clusters gathered
Whose eyes avoided me
   When I raced frantically past,

Guided by their silence
   To the narrow tumbledown lane
In which singing blades
   Had ended their intimate work.

I knew they would get you
   Down some alleyway like that,
Ringed by silent gangs
   With both the exits blocked.

You never knew fear
   And that caused your death,
Trusting the familiar
   You roared into their trap.

You'd become an exile
   Stranded in your native city
Whose police eyed you,
   Distrustful of neutrality.

The dealers watched,
   Hating your open contempt
And kids growing up
   Dreamt of your motorbike

Secretly dismantled
   For clean needles and deals.

They hovered, waiting,
  Every morning you left me.

One Friday a money-lender
  Arrived menacingly at our flat,
Hunting an old neighbour.
  You grabbed his black folder,

Releasing the pages
  To scatter down into the yard,
Like fugitive moons
  From an exploding white star

Which would eclipse us
  Within its relentless orbit.
I watched those pages
  Flutter into death warrants

That you just ignored.
  In sleep I saw charred corpses
I could not recognise
  And clutched you till you woke,

Begging you to leave
  While we still might escape.
You smiled back at me,
  Listening to late night traffic,

And said, in wonderment,
  Darling, I've finally come home,
Then curled against me
  As if love could save us from harm.

*

My lament for you, Arthur Cleary,
  And for the life which we led,
For your laughter given freely
  From those blood stained lips,

In that year we lived as one,
  Without priest or registrar
To bless the ringlets of sweat
  That tied our limbs together.

I will not put on black
  And spin out my life in mourning,
I will breathe your name
  On the lips of another's children,

Like a secretive tongue
  They will carry in their hearts
To the foreign factories
  In which their lives will pass.

When loud sirens scream
  Across the European continent,
And they walk into dawn
  Towards scrubbed dormitories,

They will tell the fable
  Of the one who tried to return
And ride a glinting bike
  In a final gesture of freedom,

And think of early light
  Slanted down that crooked lane,
When their ancestor fell
  And the new enslavement began.

Berlin/Dublin, 1985.

VII

from
Leinster Street Ghosts
1989

Leinster Street Ghosts

(i.m. Harry Sheridan)

This was never meant
    To be how our paths fork:
Me leaning my head against
    The bare plaster-work
To catch the murmuring
    Of curious mourners,
Crowding the smoky parlour
    Where you reluctantly sat
When the wind was too cold
    To haunt the front step.
You divided your days there
    Between opera and talk shows,
With ears on the alert
    For any caller to our door.

Harry, you were supposed
    To miss me when I left,
Not leave me stranded,
    Aware of how you felt
Pierced by loneliness on nights
    When poker hands were dealt
Across our kitchen table,
    And laughter echoed
With the clink of glasses
    To where you stood alone:
An eighty-year-old widower,
    Your head caressing stone

As you suffered, listening
    To friends who had gathered.

Behind you, the white dot
    On your ancient television
Reminded you it was late
    And darkness beckoned
Up a stairway thronged with absence.
    How often did you hang your cap
Over the brass bedpost
    And suddenly hear voices
Spill out into the garden
    Of our rented house next door?

You'd curse yourself for giving up,
    When you might have appeared
From nowhere at your gate –
    Like the ghost you have become –
To snatch one final chat
    With some sleepy gambler
Who would always remember
    The wave, as he cycled home,
Of Harry Sheridan:
    A fierce man to talk,
    A King amongst his words.

1989

Owen

There are childhood jungles
    Of potato stalks,
Cropped ghosts of gardens
    That I have lost,
Where you belong
    Beside a rooted fork,
Weeding laden beds
    Until after dusk,
Coaxing a damp bonfire
    And breathing in
The reek of green leaves
    And of paraffin.

A dog barks beneath apple boughs,
    Rhode Island Reds scatter
As hands seek a treasure trove
    Of warm eggs under straw.
A kitchen door is framed in light
    As the evening dissolves
In a chorus of rural accents.
    The scent of baking wafts
From your hard-won *lebensraum*
    To this floodlit balcony
Where I wait for news of you,
    My favourite uncle.

How you would love this sight,
    A cold nocturnal breeze,
The creaking limbs of sycamore
    Softened by amber light.
I start a cigarette for you,
    Inhale as slowly as I can,

When its light has burnt out
      Your life will have gone.
For now you are corralled
      In a hospital gown,
Hands plucking at blankets
      Frantic to go home.

"I'm dying and I don't want to."
      Who can reply to such torment,
Except to hope for some garden
      Where leaves are never burnt
Like the lining on your lung
      After radiation treatment.
Perhaps there is only oblivion:
      I just know that moments ago
Your drugged eyes suddenly shone,
      Mesmerised and wide-open,
As you named long dead women
      As if they gathered in welcome.

Soon it will be spring
      In the gardens of Finglas,
Lilac and cherry blossom
      Will bloom in your absence.
Another child will run
      Home from the chip shop,
Moist beads of vinegar
      Staining his jacket,
His thoughts already turned
      Towards London or New York,
Beyond from this city terrace
      Your country hands bought

With money orders sent
      From an English car plant.

Rhubarb and cabbage sown
Before reboarding the boat,
In expectation of a time
When you would finally return.
How could you have known
Emigration would start again?
Fewer neighbours will lean
Over garden walls this spring,
Fewer drinkers will argue
Across Martins' pub table,

Fewer children will be left
To plant shrubs in your place,
The lilac will wither
Unplucked on the branch.
Above me a late jet
Winks one bloodshot eye,
Bearing an aisle of young faces
In a updated newsreel.

I try to cup the hot butt,
The cigarette is finished,
Worms of ash scatter
Down onto the car park.
The telephone is throbbing,
I step through the door:
It takes me a life-time
To lift the receiver.

1986

The Dreamer's Infidelity

It disturbed me last night:
 Your face pressed so close
  To mine as you spoke:
  'I could use a man.'
 I had only one condom left,
 If I used it she would know:
  Yet I so desperately wanted
 To taste what I shouldn't know
Before my chance was gone.

The dream fuses into a blur:
 All I know is that I wake
  Aching for the touch
  Of what I cannot expect,
 Still sensing my hand close
 To your upturned breast.
  I feel so overwhelmed
  I cannot help myself,
 There seems nothing I wouldn't do
To have known you just once

Before you vanish into a future
 In which I have no place.
  Already it is too late:
  Your wing-beats will shade
 Half the globe in shadow
 Before I'm washed awake, dazed,
  Beside this woman I love –
 Like a fish gasping for breath,
 Hating myself for lying there

Still unable to forget
Your thighs I will never touch
Your milkwhite undulating neck.

1987

The Buried Stream

There is a past
    You could not fathom
Which is present,
    Which keeps waiting
For you to chance on
    In your imagination.

    Young man,
These unsought words
    Are not yours.
Before your fathers came
    We dwelt here.
You did not invent us.

    Towards evening
We came forth to linger
    In this clearing
Beside the overhung river,
    Where branches swam
In beryl trout pools
    Now piped underground.

We imagined your future:
    This apartment block
With its amber-lit car park
    Below which our bones rot,
And you at your table
    Hurriedly writing down
On this torn envelope
    Words not your own.

1986

The Ghosts of the Suburb

A sapling snapped in the undergrowth,
A startled badger fled:
A brown rat camouflaged itself
When your first footsteps fell.
I welcomed you as I had welcomed
Migrating birds and blundering elk,
And carved my name to be hewn out
Of ice-scooped ridges and hillocks
By your club-laden ancestors
Who stealthily moved inland.

I found the space for them
To pierce my soil and bear forth
Rough lines of wheat and children,
Wood smoke snaking through branches,
Beeswax light seductive in the evening.

A shrill bell to banish druids,
Fawns at the forest edge
Searched for slaughtered parents
As the otter retreated and the fox.
You took me as if I was your chattel,
Drawing boundaries, taming my flocks.
Only occasionally did I flex
My sluggish sinews of water:
A lamb found floating in a drain,
A white-skinned daughter drowned
Whom I had loved to watch bathing.
The after-image of burning pitch
Reflecting down each river bank
Where men ran crying her name

As she swayed in a lapping pool,
With her goose-pimpled clitoris
Splayed open under my tongue.
Otherwise I let you imagine
That you ruled my haunted acres.

For centuries you came for shelter
Like hundreds of shivering creatures:
Golden crops, blackened crops,
Seed thrown from a wicker basket.
When, along a track where rabbits fled,
You laid the foundations of streets.
I even welcomed those regimented lights,
The laughter of daughters lining bus routes.

The paintwork hadn't time to crack
On your fortified ranks of terraces
Before others moved here into towering flats,
Poorer than you but seeking that shelter
I'd given for centuries to beast and man.
You built high walls to carve me asunder
And then
          You took my name and changed it,
As if it were a cancer on your lips,
Smeared it on my left breast to epitomise the poor,
While you branded on my flank a foreign place-word.

You think my ghosts are banished
Beyond your double-glazed cul-de-sacs,
But tonight, while you consume capsules
To hasten the rush towards morning,
Not only your fridges are murmuring.
A spectral brown rat scuttles
Across fallow acres of Axminster

To slip past your moonlit banisters.
In brightly painted plywood cots
The children you watch over sleep
As plastic beads of doll's eyes
Blink with fright at the intruder.
He breathes the placename you've cursed
In a high pitched squeal of syllables,
Terrifying your tamed dogs who bark
Along avenues crucified by shadows.
His heartbeat ticks in a Disney clock
Like a ghost who will not be exorcised.

My streams still sing in hallow pipes,
My clay heart beats in exile,
Beneath concrete my worms crawl,
With mouths anticipating your skull.
Ghosts of startled badgers flee
Through walls of sleeping terraces,
A brown rat camouflages itself
Amid soft toys in the nursery;
Thirty centuries of disease
Incubating between his paws
Toying with the streaked hair
Of an infant's Cindy doll.

Do not imagine yourself safe
When you disregard my laws.

1986

After Words

Why should we be gone
   Just because we are dead
And you inhabit our home,
   Converting the coal shed
We'd stooped in for cinders
   In the hoarfrost of winter?

Your workmen have hammered
   Out new window-frames,
Your long-haired boy races
   In sweatshirt and sandals
Where our son played games
   In callipers and stiff laces.

With ten shilling notes saved
   On nights when we walked
Through streets where rich folk
   Gazed out from restaurants:
Living on black tea and bread,
   We scanned a post office book,
Willing it to grow like we'd seen
   Our fathers will winter crops.
Finally we paid our deposit
   To the estate manager
And momentarily held the deeds
   Of this house like a missal.

Years of white shirts and red ties,
   Sons kneeling to serve Mass,
Of Sunday wafers of ice-cream
   Sliced by the wrinkled woman

Whose cottage beside the stream
    Had a fridge in her parlour.

Four times we pushed our pram
    Past yew trees that stretched
Across the cemetery railings
    Where our bodies now rest.
A gravedigger rakes the gravel
    Every last week of October
When the payment is sent
    From our daughter in Leicester,
Whose neatly written envelopes
    We waited for each Christmas,
Bearing photos of grandchildren
    With English accents.

Why should we be gone
    Just because we are dead?
Where else have we to go
    When this was our home?
Between June and October
    One cortege followed another,
Lines of mourners and flowers
    Pausing outside this door.
That eternity of dislocation
    Waiting for God to come,
Bewildered by his absence
    Till a tunnel of light shone
Which we felt ourselves ascend,
    As giddy as at Christmas-time
When the neighbours came in
    And we'd drink Babycham.

Yet no gates of gold beckoned
    Where Seraphim sang,

No dead faces we once knew
    Floated past in welcome.
We found ourselves trapped
    Between bricks and mortar,
Watching auctioneers check
    These walls for dry rot.

Our wireless with its settings
    For Hilversum and Cairo
Lay beside the shoehorn
    And the woodwormed table,
Exposed for three weeks
    In a skip on the pavement.
Footsteps muddied the lino
    We'd always kept polished,
Eyes sneered in the bathroom
    At our wooden toilet seat.

Weeks of silence followed,
    Bare floorboards, musty rooms,
Till the afternoon you came.

    One night in a biscuit tin
Concealed behind shutters
    You found fifty pound notes
Wrapped up with scapulars
    In a surgical stocking,
For Masses for our souls
    To be said to half-seven
To the dwindling congregation
    Who might prize us into heaven.
You unfurled them in your hands
    With such revulsion,
Then made jokes with friends
    Over chilled white wine.

What have you done with them,
  Strangers in our midst?
You have stolen our key to heaven,
  We are stranded without it.

1987

Beechwood

I want it back:
Your floorboards where I slept
        In a youthful stupor,
Not bothering to get undressed.
        I want to wake
Wrecked beneath a blanket,
        The aftertaste
Of whiskey scorching my throat,
        With my limbs –
Immersed in magnified light
        Drenching through
Those latticed panes of glass –
        Stiffly reviving
With numb, exhausted happiness.

I want the hunger
Of expectation in night clubs,
        The meal mirrored
In a waitress's eyes lit by drugs.
        I want to shuffle
For Seven and Five Card Stud
        While water pipes
Breathe through the lips of gamblers.
        I want to squander
Every penny for the taxi fare,
        Be forced to walk
Past dawn-lit whores on the canal
        Back to your flat
To toss pebbles at the window.

I want to screw
Carelessly in some slanted attic
        Where low windows
Project a fanlight of branches,
        And parties spin past
Like discarded fireworks
        Through every tier
In a warren of plywood bedsits.
        I want to plunder
A girl's black bike from the hall,
        To collide with
A tree trunk on the pavement,
        And leave braincells
Strewn like momentoes over the city.

        Then, when it's over,
I want to wake again in Beechwood,
        On that same floor
Between your bed and wardrobe,
        And open my eyes,
Hypnotised by immaculate light –
        Like a child again
Boxed in a dark confessional
        When the slot opens
And a mesh of light cascades
        Onto his celibate face
And devoutly raised eyes,
        With his throat ablaze
From a hunger he will never satisfy.

1987

A Memory: Madeleine Stuart

Down two blue furlongs of tar
     She watched the postman descend,
Certain by the outline of his bag
     The manuscript had been returned.
After she placed it on the table
     She walked out into the garden
Where Francis knelt among rows of plants,

Sensing, by the pause of his hands,
     That he knew without her speaking.
Until darkness stole their shape
     She kept a vigil at his back
As his fingers nursed the soil,
     Waiting for an Aztec sunflower
To raise its gold head in redemption.

1986

Wishbone

Do not be afraid, my oldest friend,
  To send a sign that you are gone:
    In the malaise after your funeral

    Visit me unexpectedly some morning,
  Your face behind mine in the mirror,
Glimpsed for an instant, startlingly young.

1988

Leinster Street

I

Let us wake in Leinster Street,
    Both of us still twenty-six,
On a spring Monday in 1985.
    We lie on, relaxed, illicit,
Listening to the melody below
    Of friends cooking breakfast.

Flaking paint on the lattice,
    Old wire, crumbling stone,
The silos of the abandoned mill
    Framed by windows which open
Onto flowers that are lodged
    Between bricks in the lane.

And no need for us to rise
    For one more drowsy hour:
Lie on with me in that moment
    When you were still too shy
To dress yourself while I watched
    Your limbs garbed in light.

II

In those rooms five years passed
    In a single drawn-out breath,
Before we plunged into new lives.
    Remember how the ceiling wept
Beneath each rafter in the winter,
    The rustle of cards that crept

Up unlit stairways after midnight.
    May some tenant of the future
Turn when switching out his light
    And, framed by the doorway, glimpse
The phosphorescence of our lives
    Still glowing with this happiness.

1989

VIII

New Poems
1990–1998

Botanic Gardens Triptych

I: *"Algae Hibernicae"*
(Seaweeds collected by William McCalla)

Your fingers press samples of seaweed down,
In Roundstone, Connemara, the year of 1845,
With no sign yet of how neighbours will die.

You cross the rocks, a schoolmaster's son,
Transcribing into Latin from your Gaelic tongue
The species of each algae that you find.

In the Botanic Gardens, where your work will rest,
David Moore bends among flowering beds to spot
A fungal blight beneath rows of potato stalks.

Soon cholera will plunder your young breath.
Neighbours will disperse like sycamore sepals
Into open pits, coffin ships and work houses;

Or slave on rich follies that will never match
The Curvilinear Range Glasshouse rising above
The belly of this city, swollen with hunger,

Where those begging at the gates for bread
Will watch workmen cough typhus onto glass
Curving over plants stolen from tropical slopes.

And, in the herbarium, a space will be found
For the seaweeds you press with such hope
Between the pages of your *Algae Hibernicae*,

While barefoot children laugh on the rocks
Where flies will soon buzz about their mouths,
Green from seaweed and half-digested grass.

1994

II: The Midnight Watch

The herbarium drawer opens: liverwort and moss
Soak themselves afresh as when plucked
By A. P. Fanning off some hillside rock.

A dismantled bell rings, furnace sparks ignite,
Ants scurry beneath meteorite storms of acorns
As Paul Boshill mows around him at ninety-one.

Can you hear perambulators creak beneath yews,
Orchid petals parachute again to their deaths,
A child's cry forever lost in an August gale?

And every tree felled by long-saw or storm,
Every horse that stomped in the frost at dawn,
Each galaxy of leaves that once burst forth

Surges again through life in the time it takes
The drowsy nightwatchman to turn his face,
Unsure if something stirred in the undergrowth.

1994

III: Polygonum Baldschuanicum:
Russian Vine or Mile-A-Minute

One day it shall be you who will inherit
    House and shed and every crevice
In every penthouse, lift-shaft and billet.

Rooftops of tangled blossoms entwining,
    Tendrils glistening in rooms
That light and voices have long forsaken.

And no place will have escaped your noose
    Of leaves and shoots: a green python
Choking our civilisation, like a dozing goose
    Who forgot to sleep with one eye open.

1994

Poem for a Newspaper

I

Imagine this poem, boxed
   Among columns of newsprint,
      In a paper you've half-read.

Tonight is when you move
   Into your first house.
      How eerie the rooms seem:

With bare light bulbs,
   Strips of unfaded carpet
      Like sunken graves that mark

Where furniture once stood.
   Paint tins have been stacked
      Beside the spare mattress.

Tomorrow new carpets will arrive.
   You finger the knife and tacks,
      Already hearing in your mind

The trundle of a child's tricycle,
   Bare feet, muffled by underlay,
      Racing to attend your arrival home.

It is midnight when you start.
   This poem is the sole witness
      To you ripping old carpets apart

To make the rooms feel your own.
　　The house is naked for you to possess,
　　　　Yet all you can do is lay newspaper down.

II

Decades pass and you will be dead
When somebody lifts those carpets.

The house stripped bare as they glance
Through these verses you half-began,

Trying to fathom your unknown life,
Your thoughts as you worked, through them.

1993

Tell Them I Came and No One Answered

The back gate was tangled with Russian vine.
A weak light glimmered in the bathroom.
Our old hedge had caved in to block the lane
And buckle the rusted Corporation railing.

I heard your boneshaker rattle behind me,
Our children haul paraffin from Kelly's shop.
A black cat stared from the shed rooftop.

'Tell them I came and no one answered.'

The cement path was rinsed by blue moonlight
As I stood by our windowsill and watched
Strangers play with the child they were bathing.

The nuns claimed that children in the wards
Would disturb patients preparing to meet God;
You brought me in their scrubbed photograph
Dressed in what I guessed were mourning clothes.

I promised to slip home down the back lane
And surprise them some night at the Rosary:
Their excited cries upon hearing my voice again.

1992

April Bright

April Bright rushes unseen
  Though stippled wallpaper
    Where a doorway had been.

Past the bend on the stairs
  In a blaze of evening light,
    She flicks back bobbing hair

From her radiant features,
  And runs towards the wide
    Open arms of her future,

With eyes so alert
  And limbs as virginal
    As the handkerchief

In the breast pocket
  Of her school uniform –
    Which she could not use

To veil her forehead
  When she wished to light
    A candle in the chapel,

Because of dark blood
  Staining the fibres
    That she had coughed up.

1991

Taking My Letters Back

(For S. F.)

The envelope rests like a coffin
  In the glove compartment.
I have parked at this turning
  By the old schoolhouse
Where artists cheerfully work
  In batik and poverty.

Beyond an acre of stacked rafters
  Salvaged from some asylum,
Past a honeycomb of tyre tracks
  I glimpse the mobile home
Where you live at ninety-one
  Among the building young.

I am taking my letters back
  In case they are burnt
In the bonfire after your death.
  I re-read them last night
And it did not seem like you
  Who was facing oblivion,

Surrounded by this activity,
  But that excited youth
Typing poems onto carbon paper
  Over an extinct ribbon,
And hitching lifts to share them
  In your candlelit caravan.

When I hear that you have gone
  I'll recall driving off at dawn
In the same steadfast silence
  With which you carried home,
To your wild woodland lawn,
  The ashes of your son.

Wexford, 1994

'Last Songs' by Francis Ledwidge

I hold this book you have never seen,
Published by Herbert Jenkins, London,
In the armistice of nineteen eighteen,

Before those of your limbs they could salvage
Were re-buried in grave Number 5, Row B,
The Second plot, Artillery Wood Cemetery.

When I was younger you were like a brother,
At night I wanted your ghost to haunt me.

Now, reading you again, what I most reject
Are the faults I abhor in my younger self.

We have so little left in common, Frank:
Yet I know that when it comes my turn
To venture down the tunnel of the unknown

You will be among the hallucinogenic ranks
Of shuffled faces crowding in to welcome.
Finally we shall recognise each other.

1996

Poem for a Sculpture in Finglas

(Sculpted by Leo Higgins from bronze casts of local people's hands in the shape of a raven in flight.)

These were not twigs with which I built my nest
But the knuckles and joints of a thousand hands:
Nails whitened by flour, blackened by coal dust,
Fingers of schoolgirls, grandparents, husbands,
Caught in a bronze fist and then cast into flight.
My ribcage was the rafters of a thousand terraces
Where I nestled in the eaves amid a maze of lights:
Each life beating like a secret in my breast.

1990

Ash Wednesday

From a distance the entire city
  Wears a bullet hole in its forehead,
Except for the track-suited children,
  Racing beneath the builders' cranes,
With plastic pistols in their hands.

The Lenten box squats on the counter,
  Embossed with the starving child
Staring into the blue photo lens
  As though the click of the shutter
Would blow its shaved head asunder.

The age of the world is twelve.
  It has nothing left to give up.
Children inside the limbs of men
  Swarm out, screaming about God,
And masturbate with their guns.

Ash Wednesday, 1993

Blasphemy

(i.m. Father Brendan Smyth)

They carried Christ home on their tongues:
Those honest women who laboured in the dark
Of frozen byres, never breaking their fast
As they ironed white shirts for the sons

They took pride in, serving at communion.
They were driven home from Kilnacrott,
Parched for tea to slacken their thirst,
Before the special Sunday dinner was cooked.

Each mother carried Christ on her tongue,
Fortified by the Host placed on her lips,
That bore the stain of a priest's fingertips,
Smeared with the excrement of children.

1995

Ireland: 1967

Nothing much happened around here back then:
The young were an array of foreign stamps
Illuminating the mantelpieces of lonely men
Waiting for crops, death or drainage grants.

But occasionally men would crane their necks
At the distant drone of helicopter blades
Soaring against the sun, in a glinting speck

Of hope that sods might be turned, bricks laid
By Brylcreamed Gods stepping from Mercs
To conjure factories and sink mine-shafts.

The future flew beyond them, immeasurably perfect:
They could imagine his mohair suit and handclasp,
As they gazed, gape-mouthed, convincing themselves
That the Minister himself had just swept past.

1995

On a Train in England

(For Dylan Michael Gwyn Jones)

You will never know of this moment:
The Northern landscape of England passing
As a stranger pauses, slightly reticent
To ask the woman if she wished for children.

He cannot tell if her smile belies hope or regret,
The train surges on, towns pass.
Her hands are folded, feeling for each secret
Flutter of your feet next to her heart.

1998

Balustrade, Clonturk Home
for the Blind

Gulls cried downstream, cable wires hummed,
Barefoot errandboys contracted gangrene
Running with open sores through horses' dung.

Rebellion crackled in blue sparks down tramlines
As workmen dismantled you on Sackville Bridge
For shipment in sections to the Home for the Blind.

Ceilings here are high, curtains rarely drawn.
People pass the balustrade as old men emerge
With books of raffle tickets and tapping canes.

Pausing in the still air, only they can sense
The screech of gulls, patriots and urchins,
Timber ships creaking past the tenements.

1998

Going Home for Christmas

Mohill and Abbeyfeale, Kinvara and Rathvilly
Were the hometowns of girls for whom my feelings
Went silently unrequited in the branch libraries.

I'd requisition road atlases, shelved at 912.415,
And trace their weekly home-coming by private bus
To Louisburgh and Ferns, remote realms of Offaly.

Each girl's place-name in turn so captivated me
That now, passing road signs for them in December,
I cannot see narrow streets of small shop windows,

Advertising local bands and Christmas Club Specials.
It's the effervescent features of young girls I see,
With strands of tumble-weed hair illuminating

The roadway, sweeping back, twisting around corners
To light up damp alleys and bustling main streets
Where buses from the past stop for them to alight

Into the arms of loved ones and lovers at Christmas:
In Mohill and Abbeyfeale, Kinvara and Rathvilly:
Ghosts from 1980, in their first flame of beauty.

1997

Martha

I found the box of old albums,
Blew dust off a disused needle,

Tom Waits began to sing 'Martha'.
Once again I was twenty-four,

The pull of hash and tobacco,
Cheap white wine at my elbow

At the window of your bedsit
In the dust-filled August light.

A needle bobbing over warped vinyl
One final time before we stroll

Down to bars where friends gather.
Decks to be shuffled, numbers rolled,

Blankets bagged on some dawn-lit floor.
Our lives are just waiting to occur

As we linger in the infinity it takes
For the voice of Tom Waits to fade.

1995

i.m. Rory Gallagher

(for Keith Donald)

There came a time on those summer nights
      When a free house had been found,
And a cheap stereo rigged with strobe lights
      That froze each moment in your mind.

You just knew when the crowd had waned
      And the wasters had long gone
That soon the wised-up boys who remained
      Would put Rory Gallagher on.

16.6.1995

Temple Street Children's Hospital

I

This is your territory, I brought you here:
Shoddy tenement windows where washing flaps,
Crumbling lanes where cars get broken for parts.

There is an archway beneath which we passed –
Like the one above which you shared a flat
With your sisters up from Monaghan for work

In a war-becalmed Dublin. Surely you must once
Have gazed up, puzzled by how the years since
Had landed you here with a son, a stuttering misfit,

Unable to pronounce the most simple of words,
A bright penny whose cloud you'd never see lift
As you fretted, unaware of how close death hovered.

The speech therapist's office had fancy toys and books
And a special mirror which allowed me to be watched.
The waiting room contained a white merciless clock

Which ticked off the final hours we spent alone,
Gazing down at a garden where I yearned to walk,
Trapped indoors by the shame of my garbled tongue.

II

I stand outside that hospital in Nerney's Court,
At Kelly's Row where an blacksmith once worked,

And no logic can explain why you feel this close,
Why I see us in the mother and child who pass,

Or how, as I age, I slowly become your son,
Gazing through your eyes with incomprehension.

I was too young to have known you, so it makes no sense
That every passing year only deepens your absence.

1996

Millbourne Winter

Three-quarter moon and a scatter of stars,
A frost that is not yet hard,
A dog's clear bark, a chemist's sign
Flashing in cold blue, on and off.

A cat crouching above the old man's shop
Which sold knick-knacks and colouring books,
And the warmth pulsing through my legs
That have left the bed where we made love.

1993

Holotropic Botanicus

I close my eyes to find before me
  A wooden door with a silver handle,
    Which I feel unable to open,
      Which opens by itself inwardly.

Beyond it, a nightscape of stars
  Weakens down to the glimmer
    Of a sweating pane of glass,
      Curved within corroding girders.

The Waterlily House of the Botanic Gardens;
  My son's face moisted in the sultry light,
    We are seated by the plopping waterwheel
      And we are smiling across at each other.

I only realise as the scene is dissipating
  That I am him and the tall figure my mother,
    Goldfish flit through the green water
      And we are smiling across at each other.

1993

Three Seasons for My Sons

I: Walking in Spring with My Sons

Let us search for tractors and motorbikes,
Let the evening be bewitched with promise,
The man who chains the gates of the park
A distant sandman not to be evoked yet.

And let me share your eyes as we look
For birds nesting in sycamore and ash;
Let your fingers nestle in my palms
As you point in wonder at trailers and trucks,

And we stride with such tremendous purpose
After our shadows stretching along the path.

Griffith Park, Drumcondra, 1994

II: Collecting Chestnuts with My Sons, September, 1995.

These lines are written because I cannot tell
What permutations for us all may lie ahead,
And so I wish to record for you the fact
That we collected, in the space of an hour

And within one hundred yards of our house,
Three hundred and ninety-one fallen chestnuts,
Many still cocooned in thick, prickly shells,
The others glinting from the drenched grass.

When another three decades have passed
Will children still hunt here for chestnuts?
Shall these boughs have long been felled

By freak storm, melt-down or pestilence,
Or will thirty new rings circle their hearts
As excited children crack shells on the path?

There is so little we can honestly predict,
Except that children inevitably look back
At the modernity parents felt they lived in

To see how life was backward and simpler then.
So much of your lives will have already occurred,
Such roots set down across an altered world,

That these lines may be all you have to recall
This ordinary Sunday, after a night of squalls,
As you raced beneath leaves still dripping wet
To cram every pocket of your father's jacket

With the polished whorls of smooth chestnuts;
My two beautiful sons, aged three and aged five,
Scampering off again to plunder the opened husks
That waited to be spied by your flawless eyes.

24.9.1995

III: *The Constellations of Drumcondra*

Who knows what records you may break
   Or what goals the world will set you,
But there's no voyage you'll undertake
   With a purpose so clear and absolute
As this search in the December twilight
   For the sparkle of lit trees in windows.

How many shall I count, walking tonight,
   Wrapped up for the cold with my boys?
Breaking our record of two hundred and six
   Leaves neither of you satisfied,
Knowing there must be one last cul-de-sac
   Whose array has not yet been spied.

Cities won't always have seasons like this:
   Chestnuts like manna in the autumn grass,
Blackberries growing wild in the colleges,
   And candles in windows in the wintry dark.
You will grow older, losing your innocence,
   And, with luck, eventually gaining it back.

But may you never lose the sense of resolve
   With which you both grip my hand
Beneath a skyline of stars foretelling frost,
   And lead me around a penultimate bend
Onto a street alive with leaping swordfish
   And acrobats from the fantastical land

Which spills over from your imagination.
   There, amid the constellations of Drumcondra,
You eventually reach the magical number

Which, by unspoken consent, allows us to turn,
Astronomers, explorers returning from afar
  To glimpse the final lit window which is home.

December, 1996